NATURE WATCH

BUTTERFLIES
and MOTHS

John Farndon

Consultant: Michael Chinery

LORENZ BOOKS

C O N

First published in 1999 by Lorenz Books

© Anness Publishing Limited 1999

Lorenz Books is an imprint of Anness Publishing Limited, .
Hermes House, 88–89 Blackfriars Road, London SE1 8HA.

Published in the USA by Lorenz Books, Anness Publishing Inc.,
27 West 20th Street, New York, NY 10011; (800) 354–9657.

This edition distributed in Canada by Raincoast Books, 8680
Cambie Street, Vancouver, British Columbia, V6P 6M9.

ISBN 1 85967 612 X

A CIP catalogue record for this book is
available from the British Library

Publisher: Joanna Lorenz
Managing Editor, Children's Books: Sue Grabham
Senior Editor: Nicole Pearson
Editors: Simon Beecroft; Nicky Barber
Designer: Vivienne Gordon
Picture Researcher: Liz Heasman
Illustrators: Julian Baker, Stuart Carter, Vanessa Card,
David Webb
Special Photography: Kim Taylor
Production Controller: Ann Childers
Editorial Reader: Richard McGinlay

Printed and bound in Singapore

10 9 8 7 6 5 4 3 2 1

**The butterflies and moths used in this book are often
described using their common English names first, followed
by their Latin names in *italic*. Where a butterfly or moth does
not have a common name, only its Latin name is given.**

PICTURE CREDITS
b=bottom, t=top, c= centre, l= left, r= right
H. Angel: 17bl&r; ARDEA LONDON/P. Morris: 60tr; BRIDGEMAN
ART LIBRARY: 4cr (The legend of Cupid and psyche by Angelica
Kauffman [1741-1807] Museo Civico Rivoltello), 55bl ("Etain,
Helen, Maeve and Fand, Golden Deirdre's Tender Hand".
Illustration from 'Queens' by J. M. Synge by Harry Clarke [1890-
1931] Private collection); M. Chinery: 26tl, 31cl, 36tr, 39cl, 46tl,
47bl, 48tl, 60bl; BRUCE COLEMAN/I. Arndt: 40bl, 50c; /J.
Brackenbury: 55bl; /B. Coleman: 54bl; /G. Cubitt: 36cr; /J. Dore:
50bl; /P. Evans: 45bl, 51bl; /M. Fogden: 16tl, 44bl; /B. Glover:
33cl; /Sir J. Grayson: 23tl; /D. Green: 50bl; /F. Labhardt: 10cr,
49tc; /G. McCarthy: 8br, 39bl; /L. Claudio Marigo: 44br, 60cr;
/A. Purcell: 8bl, 33tr, 43tr, 53br, 54br, 55cl; /M. Read: 61tl; /J.
Shaw: 28tl; /J. Taylor: 49tl; /K. Taylor: 9cl, 21br, 23br, 27tl&cr,
50tr, 52br, 61bl; /C. Varndell: 55tr; /C. Wallace: 53tr, 61cr; /W. C.
Ward: 48br; /R. Williams: 52bl; Mary Evans: 13cr, 23cl, 27cl,
31tl; FLPA/R. Austing 40br; /B. Borrell: 12bl; /R. Chittenden:
47tl; /C. Newton: 47tr; /F. Pölking 34tr; /I. Rose: 41cr; /L. West:
12cl, 47br; /R. Wilmshurst: 37cl; GARDEN/WILDLIFE MATTERS/S.
Apps: 58tr; /M. Collins: 35br; /J. Fowler: 20ct; /C. Milkins: 52tl;
NATURE PHOTOGRAPHERS/Paul Sterry: 55br; NHPA/S. Dalton:
32cr; /D. Heuclin: 7cl; /PAPILIO: 8tr, 30tr; PLANET EARTH/P.
Harcourt Davies: 21tr; /G. du Feu: 11bl, 19cl, 22br, 24tl, /W.
Harris: 7tr, 21cl; /S. Hopkin: 17ct, 22bl; /K. Jayaram: 9tl; /B.
Kennery: 23cr; /A. Kerstitch: 33bc; /D. Maitland 20br;
PREMAPHOTOS WILDLIFE/K. Preston-Mafham: 4tr, 10cl, 16bl,
32bl, 35cr, 38tl&br, 39tr, 43cl; /Kim Taylor: 4bl, 5ct, 6bl, 9cr,
10tl&bc, 12br, 13cl, 18tl, 19tr&br, 21bc, 22tl, 26br, 31tr&bl, 37br,
43br, 56tl, bl&r, 57tl; VISUAL ARTS LIBRARY/Artephot, Roland:
51br; WARREN PHOTOGRAPHIC/J. Burton: 6br, 16br, 21tl, 25tr&br,
32tl, 36cl, 42bl&r, 45tl, 46br, 54tl; /K.Taylor: 5cb, 7cr&br, 9br,
11tc, 12tl&tr, 13cb, 18bl&br, 19tl, 24bl&r, 25tl, 26bl, 27tl&br,
28tl&r, 29tl, tr&cb, 31cr, 34bl&r, 37tr, 39cr, 41tl, cl&br, 42tl, 44tl,
45br, 48bl, 49br.

Thank you to Worldwide Butterflies in Sherborne, Dorset for
their help in creating this book.

INTRODUCING BUTTERFLIES AND MOTHS

BODIES, WINGS AND SENSES

LIFE CYCLE

T E N T S

Winged Beauties

Butterflies and moths are the most beautiful of all insects. On sunny days, butterflies flit from flower to flower. Their slow, fluttering flight often reveals the full glory of their large, vividly coloured wings. Moths are usually less brightly coloured than butterflies and generally fly at night. Together, butterflies and moths make up one of the largest orders (groups) of insects, called Lepidoptera. This order includes more than 165,000 different species, of which 20,000 are types of butterfly and 145,000 are types of moth. The richest variety is found in tropical forests, but there are butterflies and moths in fields, woods, grasslands, deserts and mountains in every area of land in the world – except Antarctica.

Geometrid moth
(Hypochrosis bifurcata)

Body covered in thick hair.

Feathery antennae.

▲ **MOTHS**
Most moths fly only at dusk or at night. They rest on tree trunks and leaf litter by day, where their generally drab colours make them difficult to see. Moths tend to have plump bodies covered in thick hair, and their antennae are feathery or thread-like.

▼ **RESTING BUTTERFLY**
You can usually tell a butterfly from a moth by the way it folds its wings when it is resting. A moth spreads its wings back like a tent, with only the upper sides visible. However, a butterfly settles with its wings folded flat with the uppersides together, so that only the undersides show.

Green-veined white butterfly
(Pieris napi)

Psyche and Aphrodite
The Ancient Greeks believed that, after death, their souls fluttered away from their bodies in the form of butterflies. The Greek symbol for the soul was a butterfly-winged girl called Psyche. According to legend, Aphrodite (goddess of love) was jealous of Psyche's beauty. She ordered her son Eros to make Psyche fall in love with him. Instead, Eros fell in love with her himself.

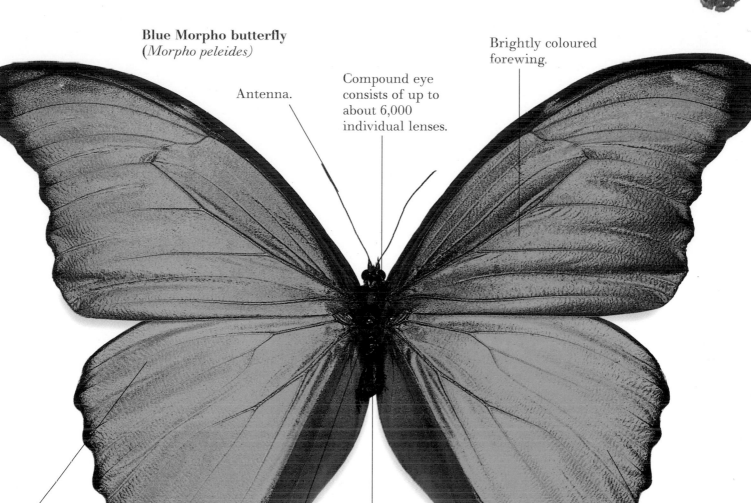

Blue Morpho butterfly
(*Morpho peleides*)

Antenna.

Compound eye consists of up to about 6,000 individual lenses.

Brightly coloured forewing.

Wing is covered in overlapping scales.

Typical slim body of a butterfly.

The hindwing is smaller than the forewing.

Tough outer coating supports the body, instead of an internal skeleton.

▲ FEATURES OF A BUTTERFLY

Butterflies tend to have brilliantly coloured wings and fly only during the day. They have slim bodies without much hair, and their antennae are shaped like clubs, with a lump at the end. However, the distinction between butterflies and moths is quite blurred, and in some countries they are not distinguished at all.

► CATERPILLARS

A many-legged caterpillar hatches from a butterfly's egg. When young, both moths and butterflies are caterpillars. Only when they are big enough do the caterpillars go through the changes that turn them into winged adults.

Privet Hawk moth caterpillar
(*Sphinx ligustri*)

Did you know? Tiger moths make high-pitched clicks at night to warn bats they taste bad.

How Butterflies Look

Butterflies vary enormously in size and shape. In regions such as Europe and the United States they range from big butterflies such as the Monarch, which has a wingspan of 10cm, to the Small Blue, which is tinier than a postage stamp. The variation among tropical species is even greater. The largest butterfly in the world is the rare Queen Alexandra's Birdwing. The female has a wingspan of 28cm, which is more than 25 times the size of the minute Western Pygmy Blue. The shape of butterfly wings can be deceptive. In photographs and drawings, butterflies are usually shown with both pairs of wings stretched out fully. However, they are not always seen like this in nature. For example, sometimes the forewings may hide the hindwings.

A male Queen Alexandra's Birdwing butterfly has brightly coloured wings.

Monarch butterfly
(Danaus plexippus)

◀ **MONARCH MIGRATIONS**
The Monarch is one of the biggest butterflies outside of tropical regions. In North America it makes long journeys, called migrations, to spend the winter in warm areas such as California, Florida and Mexico. Some Monarch butterflies fly from as far away as Canada.

▼ **COMMA BUTTERFLY**
Each species of butterfly has its own distinctive wing markings. The Comma butterfly gets its name from the small, white C or comma-shape on the undersides of its hindwings.

Comma butterfly
(Polygonia c-album)

▼ BIG AS A BIRD

The Queen Alexandra's Birdwing is a rare butterfly that lives only in the Northern Province of Papua New Guinea. Its wings are wider than those of many birds. Females can grow up to 28cm across. The male Birdwing shown in this photograph is life size.

Queen Alexandra's Birdwing butterfly
(Ornithoptera alexandrae)

The bright yellow body warns predators that the butterfly is poisonous.

Small Blue butterfly
(Cupido minimus)

▲ SMALL BLUE

The Small Blue (shown here life size) is the smallest butterfly in Great Britain. It is barely 2cm across, even when fully grown. However, the tiny Pygmy Blue butterfly of North America is even smaller with a wingspan of between 11 and 18mm.

Peacock butterfly
(Inachis io)

▶ PEACOCK EYES

The Peacock butterfly is easily identified by the pairs of markings on both the front and hindwings. These large spots look like eyes. It is one of the most common and distinctive butterflies in Europe and parts of Asia, including Japan.

▶ A TAIL OF DECEPTION

The wing shapes of butterflies can vary dramatically from species to species. Many butterflies in the family called Papilionidae have distinctive tails on their wings, a bit like swallows' tails. Some species of Swallowtail use them to confuse predators. When the wings are folded, the tails look like antennae, so a predator may mistake the butterfly's tail-end for its head.

Swallowtail butterfly
(Papilio machaon)

7

How Moths Look

American Moon moth
(Actias luna)

Like butterflies, moths come in all shapes and sizes. There is also more variety in wing shape amongst moths than amongst butterflies. In terms of size, some of the smallest species of moth have wingspans no wider than 3mm. The biggest have wings that are almost as wide as this book, for example the Hercules moth of Australia and New Guinea and the Bent-wing Ghost moth of South-east Asia. The larvae (caterpillars) of small moths may be tiny enough to live inside seeds, fruits, stems, leaves and flowers. The caterpillars of larger moths are bigger, although some do live inside tree trunks and other stems.

▲ **MOON MOTH**
The American Moon moth shows just how delicate and attractive large moths can be. Its wingspan is about 32cm and it has long, slender tails on its hindwings. When it is resting on a tree, its body and head are so well hidden by its big wings that any predatory bird will peck harmlessly at its tails. This allows the moth time to escape.

Garden Tiger moth
(Arctia caja)

▼ **ELEPHANT HAWK MOTH**
Many moths are less colourful than butterflies, but they are not all drably coloured. For example, the Elephant Hawk moth is a beautiful insect with delicate pink wings that blend in well with its favourite flowers (valerian and pink honeysuckle). However, the Elephant Hawk moth flies at night so it is not often seen in its full glory.

◄ **COLOUR RANGE**
Identifying moths can be quite difficult, as some species show a wide range of colouring. For example, many Garden Tiger moths are slightly different colours from each other. As a result of this variety, scientists often use the Garden Tiger moth for breeding experiments.

Elephant Hawk moth *(Deilephila elpenor)*

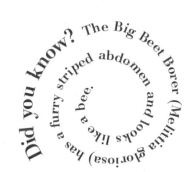

▶ INDIAN MOTH

This moth belongs to the family Pyralidae and comes from southern India. This tiny moth has a wingspan of just 2cm. The distinctive white bands on its wings break up the moth's outline and make it more difficult to spot when at rest.

Lepyrodes neptis

Did you know? The Big Beet Borer (*Melitta gloriosa*) has a furry striped abdomen and looks like a bee.

▼ WIDE WINGS

The Giant Atlas moth of India and South-east Asia is one of the world's largest moths. Only the Giant Agrippa moth of South America has wider wings, with a span of up to 30cm. Some Atlas moths grow almost as big as this entire double page when their wings are opened fully. They have shiny triangles on their wings that are thought to confuse predators by reflecting light.

Giant Atlas moth
(*Archaeoattacus edwardsi*)

▲ MANY PLUME MOTH

The beautiful feathery wings of this unusual looking moth give it its name, the Many Plume moth (*Alucita hexadactyla*). Each of its fore and hindwings is split into six slender feathery sections, or plumes.

▼ LARGE CATERPILLAR

Caterpillars have many different shapes and sizes, just like moths. The young Acacia Emperor moth is one of the biggest caterpillars. Although they are generally sausage-shaped, some caterpillars are twig-like, making them hard to see in a bush or tree.

9

Body Parts

In many ways, butterflies and moths are similar to other insects. Their bodies are divided into three parts – the head, the thorax and the abdomen. The mouth, eyes and antennae (feelers) are situated on the head. The thorax is the body's powerhouse, driving the legs and wings. The abdomen is where food is digested. Like all insects, butterflies and moths have bodies, which are covered by a tough outer shell, called an exoskeleton. However, butterflies and moths also have unique features, such as their big, flat wings and a long proboscis (tongue).

Abdomen

▲ **EGG CENTRE**

The abdomen (rear section) houses a butterfly's digestive system. It also produces eggs in female butterflies and moths, and sperm in males.

◄ **SWEET SUCKING**

This butterfly is feeding on a prickly pear cactus fruit in Mexico. Butterflies and moths feed mainly on nectar and other sweet juices. They suck them up through a long tube-like tongue called a proboscis. Butterflies and moths have no jaws.

▲ **FEEDING STRAW**

A Purple Emperor butterfly rolls out its proboscis to feed. The proboscis stretches out almost as long as its body. When a butterfly rests, it rolls up its long proboscis beneath its head. Hawk moths have the longest proboscises.

► **CONNECTED WINGS**

The forewings and hindwings of most moths overlap. Although each pair of wings is separate, they act together because long bristles on the hindwing catch on to hooks on the underside of the forewing, rather like a doorlatch.

Burnet moth with wings raised, showing the bristle linking the forewing and hindwing.

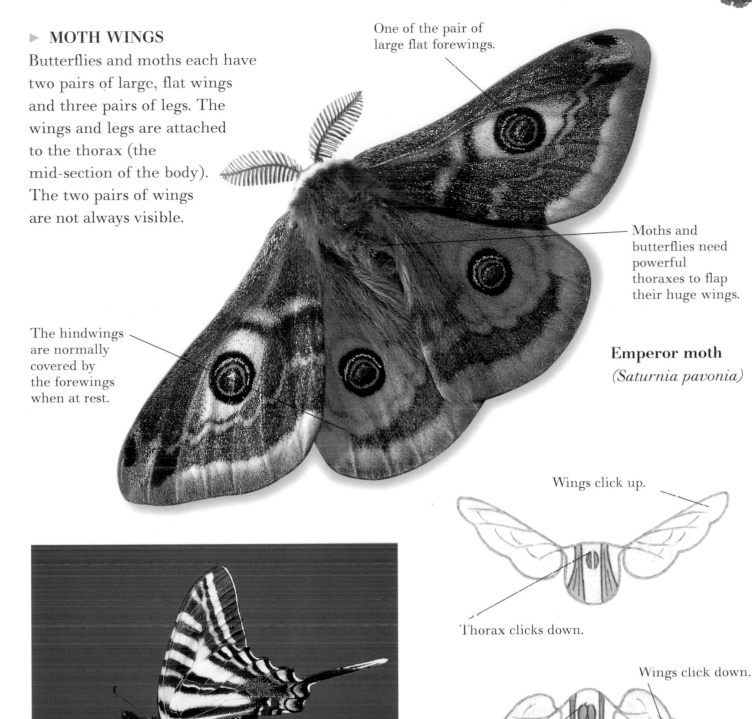

▶ **MOTH WINGS**

Butterflies and moths each have two pairs of large, flat wings and three pairs of legs. The wings and legs are attached to the thorax (the mid-section of the body). The two pairs of wings are not always visible.

One of the pair of large flat forewings.

Moths and butterflies need powerful thoraxes to flap their huge wings.

Emperor moth
(Saturnia pavonia)

The hindwings are normally covered by the forewings when at rest.

Wings click up.

Thorax clicks down.

Wings click down.

Thorax clicks up.

▲ **SENSITIVE FEET**

Moths and butterflies taste with their tarsi (feet). When they land on a flower, they will not unroll the tongue to feed unless their feet sense the sweetness of nectar. Females stamp their tarsi on leaves to decide if they are ripe for egg-laying. They will lay eggs only if the leaves release the correct scent.

▲ **FLIGHT**

The wings are joined to the thorax (mid-section). Muscles pull the top of the thorax down, making the wings flip up. Then the muscles pull the thorax in, making it thinner so the top clicks back up again, flipping the wings down.

11

European Map butterfly
(*Araschnia levana*)

Scaly Wings

The scientific name for butterflies and moths, Lepidoptera, refers to the minute scales covering their wings. *Lepis* is the Ancient Greek word for scale and *pteron* means wing. The scales are actually flattened hairs and each one is connected to the wings by a short stalk. These delicate scales give butterfly wings their amazing colours, but can rub off easily like dust. Underneath the scales, butterfly and moth wings are transparent like the wings of other insects. The vivid colours of the scales come either from pigments (coloured chemicals) in the scales or the way their structure reflects light.

▲ SCENTED SCALES

Many male butterflies have special scales called *androconia* that help them to attract mates. These scales scent the wing with an odour that stimulates females.

▲ OVERLAPPING SCALES

Tiny scales overlap and completely coat the wing. They are so loosely attached that they often shake off in flight.

▲ CELL SPACE

The areas between the wing veins are called cells. All the cells radiate outwards from one vein at the base of the wing.

Black-veined White butterfly
(*Aporia crataegi*)

▼ WING VEINS

Butterfly and moth wings are supported by a framework of veins. These veins are filled with air, nerve fibres and blood. The pattern of the veins helps to classify butterflies and moths into a number of families.

Highly visible veins of a Black-veined White butterfly.

► SCALING DOWN

A Large White butterfly takes off from a buttercup. Butterflies in flight naturally lose scales from time to time. The loss does not seem to harm some species. However, others find themselves unable to fly without a reasonable coating of scales to soak up the sun and warm up their bodies.

Did you know? The wings of the Glasswing butterfly are transparent, making it almost invisible.

◄ MORPHO WING

The metallic blue wings of the South American Morpho butterfly shimmer in the sunlight. This effect is produced by the special way the surface texture of their wings reflects light. When filmed by a video camera that is sensitive to invisible ultraviolet light, these scales flash like a beacon.

Butterfly Ball
The butterfly's fragile beauty has always inspired artists. In the 1800s, many European artists portrayed them as fairies, with human bodies and butterfly's wings.

► EYE TO EYE

The patterns of scales on some butterflies form circles that resemble the bold, staring eyes of a larger animal. Scientists think that these eyespots may have developed to startle and scare away predators such as birds. However, the eyespots on other butterflies may be used to attract mates.

Focus on

Butterflies and moths can only fly if their body temperature reaches at least 25–30°C. If they are too cold, the muscles powering the wings do not work. To warm up, butterflies bask in the sun, so that the wing scales soak up sunlight like solar panels. Night-flying moths shiver their wings to warm them instead.

Butterflies and moths fly in a different way from other insects. They fly in a similar way to birds. Most insects simply beat their wings very rapidly to move through the air. Since they can only stay aloft if they beat their wings fast enough, they soon run out of energy. However, many butterflies ripple their wings slowly up and down. Some, such as the White Admiral, can even glide on currents of air with just an occasional flap to keep them aloft. This enables them to fly amazing distances. Flight patterns vary from the fluttering of the Wood White to the soaring of the Purple Emperor butterflies. Wingbeat tends to be faster in the smaller species, with the Skipper family having the fastest wingbeat of all. Moths, such as the Hawk moths with their jet plane-like wings, fly at fast speeds in a generally straight line.

To the human eye, the wings of butterflies and moths appear simply to flap. However, freeze-frame photography reveals that the bases of the wings twist as they move up and down, so that the wing tips move in a figure of eight.

Butterflies look like clumsy fliers, but their acrobatic twists and turns enable them to escape sparrows and other predatory birds. Some moths can fly at up to 48 km/h when frightened.

14

Flight

A butterfly lifts its wings upwards.

The wings push air backwards.

The butterfly is propelled forwards.

The wings are stiff along the front edges and at the bases, but the rest of the wing is bendy. The stiff front edges of the wing give the butterfly lift, like the wings of an aircraft, as it flies forward. The flexing of the rest of the wing pushes air backwards and drives the butterfly forwards.

As the wings come down again, they provide lift to keep the butterfly up.

Butterflies in the family *Nymphalidae*, such as this Painted Lady (*Vanessa cardui*), tend to flap their wings only occasionally when in flight. They prefer to glide gracefully from flower to flower, with just the odd beat of their wings.

Senses

Butterflies and moths have a very different range of senses from humans. Instead of having just two eyes they have compound eyes, made up of hundreds or even thousands of tiny lenses. They also have incredibly sensitive antennae (feelers) which they use not only to smell food, but also to hear and feel things. The antennae play a vital part in finding a mate and deciding where to lay eggs. They may even detect taste and temperature change. Butterflies and moths have a good sense of taste and smell in their tarsi (feet), too. Moths hear sounds with a form of ears called tympanal organs. These little membranes are situated on the thorax or abdomen and vibrate like a drum when sound hits them.

▲ **ANTENNAE**
The feathery side branches on an Atlas moth's antennae increase the surface area for detecting scent, like the spikes on a TV aerial. They allow the male moth to pinpoint certain smells, such as the scent of a potential mate, at huge distances.

▲ **SMELL THE WIND**
A butterfly's antennae act like an external nose packed with highly sensitive smell receptors. They can pick up minute traces of chemicals in the air that are undetectable to the human nose.

◄ **ATTRACTIVE ANTENNAE**
Male Longhorn moths (*Adelidae*) have very long antennae. These antennae are used to pick up scent, but they also have another, very different, job. They shine in the sunlight and attract females when the males dance up and down in the afternoon.

Moth's
head

▲ HEARING BODY

Many moths have "ears"
made up of tiny
membranes stretched
over little cavities. These
ears are situated on the
thorax. When the
membranes are vibrated
by a sound, a nerve sends
a signal to the brain.
These ears are highly
sensitive to the high-
pitched sounds of bats,
which prey on moths.

A noctuid moth
showing the
position of the
ears at the rear of
the thorax.

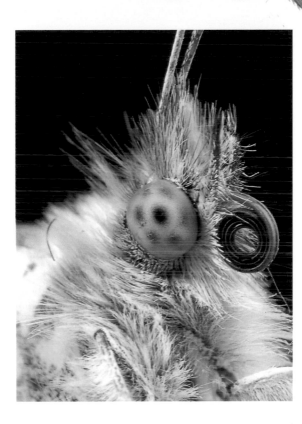

Did you know? The male Emperor moth can smell a female at 11km – upwind!

◄ MULTI-VISION

The compound eyes of an
Orange-tip butterfly are
large. The thousands of
lenses in a compound eye
each form their own
picture of the world.
The butterfly's brain puts
the images together into
one picture. Although
butterflies are quite
short-sighted, they can
see all round using their
multiple eyes.

▼ FEELING FOR FLOWERS

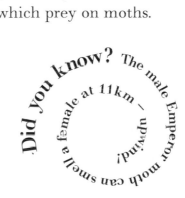

Butterflies and moths find the flowers they
want to feed on mainly
by the incredibly
sensitive sense
of smell their
antennae give
them. This
enables them
to pick up the
scent of a single
bloom from some
distance away.

▼ A CASE OF THE BLUES

Butterflies don't see flowers such as this evening
primrose the way we do,
for their eyes
are not very
sensitive to red
and yellow
light. But
they can see
ultraviolet light,
which we cannot
see. They see flowers
in the colours shown here.

Eggs

Butterflies and moths begin life as tiny eggs. After mating, some females simply scatter their eggs as they fly. However, most females seek a suitable place to fix their eggs, either individually or in batches of up to 1,000 or more. The leaves or stem of particular plants are common sites since they will provide food for the caterpillars after hatching. A female butterfly uses her sensitive antennae to locate the correct plant species. She stamps or scratches the leaves with her feet to check that the scent is right and that no other butterfly has laid eggs there before. Once she has laid her eggs, the female flies off almost straight away.

Eggs emerge through the ovipositor.

Large White butterfly
(*Pieris brassicae*)

▲ EGG OOZE

A female butterfly pushes her eggs out, one by one, through her ovipositor (the egg-laying duct at the end of her abdomen). The eggs ooze out in a kind of glue that sticks them in place as it hardens.

A Peacock butterfly's eggs, laid on the underside of a nettle leaf.

▲ RIDGED EGG

The egg of the Painted Lady butterfly has a glassy shell with elaborate ridges. The shape of the egg is fairly constant in each family.

▲ EGG SITE

A Peacock butterfly has laid her eggs on a sheltered part of the plant. This will provide them with warmth and protection, as well as food. Many butterflies and moths lay their eggs in random patterns, which improves the chances of predatory insects missing some of them.

▼ **EGGS IN CLOSE-UP**

The moth eggs shown here are red-brown and poisonous. However, most eggs are dull green or yellow in colour. This helps them to blend into their background so that they remain hidden from predators. Different types of egg are smooth, shiny or patterned.

▲ **DIFFERENT NESTS**

Some moths lay their eggs along a grass stem, so they look like the stem itself. Others lay eggs in dangling strings or in overlapping rows like tiles on a roof.

◄ **EGG SHAPES**

The eggs of a Large White butterfly are lozenge-shaped. Butterfly eggs vary in shape from the spiny balls of the White Admiral to the cones of the Silver-spotted Skipper. All have a hard shell lined on the inside with wax, which protects the developing caterpillar inside.

Newly hatched caterpillars of the Large White butterfly.

► **HATCHING EGGS**

Most butterfly eggs hatch within a few days of being laid. However, a few types of egg pass an entire winter before hatching. They hatch when temperatures begin to rise and the caterpillars stand a chance of survival. The eggs grow darker in colour just before hatching. The tiny caterpillars bite their way out from their shells. Their minute jaws cut a circle in the shell that is just big enough for the head to squeeze through.

19

The Caterpillar

Five-spotted Hawk moth caterpillar

Once a caterpillar (or larva) bites its way from the egg, it immediately begins eating. While most adult butterflies and moths survive on nectar, a caterpillar chomps it ways through leaves, fruits and stems. It grows rapidly, shedding its skin several times as it swells. Within a month, it may be fully grown and ready to change into a butterfly or moth. Caterpillars are far more numerous than adult butterflies and moths because most are eaten by predators or killed by diseases. They hide among vegetation and crevices in bark, often feeding at night to avoid danger.

Head

True legs

Thorax

Abdomen

Spine or horn at the tip of the abdomen.

Each proleg ends in a ring of crochets (hooks) that hold on to stems and leaves.

Anal proleg or clasper enables a caterpillar to cling on to plants.

◄ **CATERPILLAR PARTS**

Caterpillars have big heads with strong jaws for snipping off food. Their long, soft bodies are divided into thirteen segments. The front segments become the thorax in the adult insect and the rear segments become the abdomen.

PROLEGS ►

The caterpillar of an Emperor Gum moth (*Antheraea eucalypti*) has five pairs of prolegs (false legs) on its abdomen. All caterpillars have these prolegs, which they lose as an adult. Caterpillars also have three pairs of true legs, which become the legs of the adult.

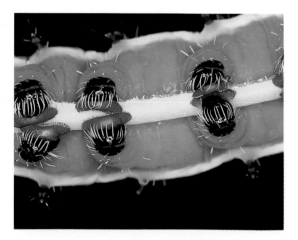

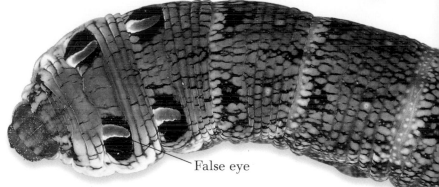

False eye

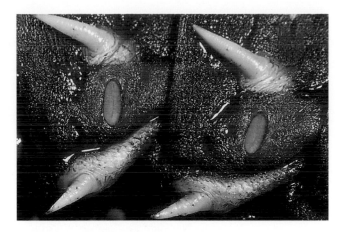

▲ **BREATHING HOLES**

A caterpillar does not have lungs for breathing like humans. Instead, it has tiny holes called spiracles that draw oxygen into the body tissues. There are several spiracles on either side of the caterpillar.

▲ **FALSE EYES**

The large eye shapes behind the head of an Elephant Hawk moth caterpillar are actually false eyes for scaring predators. In fact, caterpillars can barely see at all. They possess six small eyes that can only distinguish between dark and light.

Did you know? Caterpillars can close up their spiracles and survive underwater for hours.

◄ **CHANGING SKIN**

Every week or so, the skin of a growing caterpillar grows too tight. It then splits down the back to reveal a new skin underneath. At first the new skin is soft and stretchy. As the caterpillar sheds its old skin, it swells the new one by taking in air through its spiracles (air holes). It then lies still for a few hours while the new large skin hardens.

◄ **FLY ATTACK**

A Puss Moth caterpillar can defend itself against predators. It puffs up its front and whips its tail like a tiny dragon, before spraying a jet of poison over its foe.

SILK MAKERS ►

Peacock butterfly caterpillars live and feed in web-like tents. They spin these tents from silken thread. All caterpillars can produce this sticky liquid from the spinneret under their mouth. The silk helps them to hold on to surfaces as they move about.

Hungry Caterpillars

Caterpillars are incredible eating machines, munching their way through several times their own body weight of food in a single day. This is why they grow so rapidly. Their first meal is usually the egg from which they hatch. Once that is gone, they move on to the nearest food source. Some eat nearby unhatched eggs and a few even eat other caterpillars. Most feed on the leaves and stems of their own particular food plant. This is usually the plant on which they hatched. However, some moth caterpillars eat wool or cotton. The food is stored in the caterpillar's body and is used for growth and energy in the later stages of its development. The caterpillar stage lasts for at least two weeks, and sometimes very much longer.

Tunnel left by leaf-mining caterpillar.

▲ LEAF MINING

Many tiny caterpillars eat their way through the inside of the leaf instead of crawling across the surface. This activity is known as leaf mining. Often, their progress is revealed by a pale tunnel beneath the leaf surface.

Swallowtail butterfly caterpillar
(Papilio machaon)

Sensitive palps are located near the mouth.

The true legs are used to grip foliage.

▲ FEEDING HABITS

Caterpillars eat different food plants from those used by the adults. Swallowtail butterfly caterpillars feed on fennel, carrots and milk-parsley. Adult swallowtail butterflies drink the nectar of thistles and buddleias.

▶ IDENTIFYING FOOD

The head end of a Privet Hawk moth caterpillar is shown in close-up here. A caterpillar probably identifies food using sensitive organs called palps that are just in front of the mouth.

◀ **FAST EATERS**

Cabbages are the main food plants of the Large White caterpillar. These insects can strip a field of foliage in a few nights. This is why many farmers and gardeners kill caterpillars with pesticides. However, their numbers may be controlled naturally by parasitic wasps so long as the wasps are not killed by pesticides.

Alice in Wonderland
In Lewis Carroll's magical story Alice in Wonderland, *a pipe-smoking caterpillar discusses with Alice what it is like to change size. Carroll was probably thinking of how caterpillars grow in stages.*

▲ **PICKY EATER**
Many caterpillars feed on trees. Some, such as the Gypsy moth caterpillars, feed on almost any tree, but others are more fussy. This Cecropia moth caterpillar feeds only on willow trees.

▲ **PROCESSIONARY CATERPILLARS**
The caterpillars of Processionary moths travel to feeding areas in a neat row. They also rest together in silken nests. These insects are poisonous and so do not try to hide as others do.

Focus on

The caterpillar of the silk moth,
(*Bombyx mori*) feeds entirely on the
leaves of just one plant, the mulberry tree.
Today, silk worms do not live in the wild.
They are farmed and fed on pre-chopped
mulberry leaves.

1

Moth caterpillars ooze out a silky
liquid thread from ducts called
spinnerets. One species produces a
liquid so strong and fine that it
can be used in silk, one of the
most beautiful and luxurious of
all fabrics. This caterpillar, that of
the *Bombyx mori* moth, is known as
the silk worm. In China, it has been
cultivated for its silk for almost 5,000
years. According to legend, in about
2,700BC the Chinese princess Si-Ling-
Chi first discovered how to use the
silk worm's cocoon to make silk
thread. She was known thereafter as
Seine-Than (the Silk Goddess).

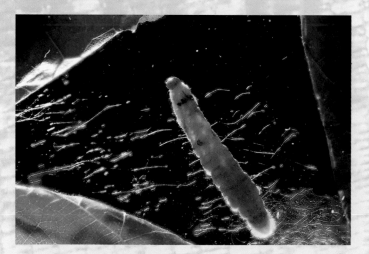

2 When the caterpillar is ready to change
into an adult moth, it finds a suitable spot
between the mulberry leaves. Once settled, it
begins to ooze silk thread from its spinneret.

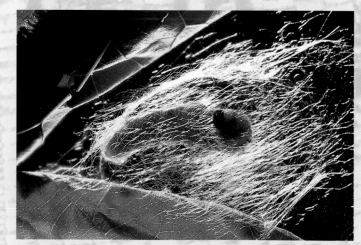

3 At first, the silk forms just a flimsy
curtain, with only a few threads strung
between the leaves. The caterpillar is still
clearly visible at this stage.

Making Silk

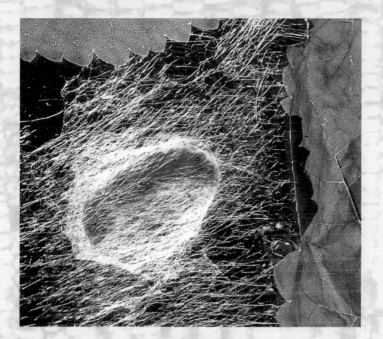

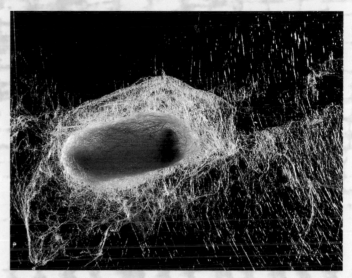

4 After a few hours the caterpillar stops running the silk between the leaves and begins to wrap itself round and round. It uses almost a kilometre of silk to completely encase itself in a cocoon of the gummy thread.

5 Inside the cocoon, the caterpillar becomes a pupa (also known as a chrysalis). This is a stage in the development of moths and butterflies when they neither feed nor move. They emerge from this stage as adult insects.

6 Only a few pupae are allowed to emerge as adult *Bombyx mori* moths for breeding. Most cocoons are plunged into boiling water, which kills the pupa and dissolves the gum on the silk. The fine silk from several cocoons is twisted together to make usable silk thread.

Pupae

Caterpillar of Large Tortoiseshell butterfly shedding its skin as it becomes a pupa.

After about a month of eating and growing, a caterpillar is ready to pupate (become a pupa). This is when it transforms into an adult butterfly or moth. Pupae are defenceless, so many moth caterpillars spin a silken cocoon around themselves for protection. Many others tunnel into the ground before pupating. Most butterfly pupae are naked, but they are generally well camouflaged or hidden in leaf litter. Cocoons look lifeless, but inside there is continuous activity as the caterpillar gradually transforms itself. This process, called metamorphosis, can take just a few days, although in some species it may be over a year before the adult insect finally emerges.

◄ **HANGING ON**
Many butterfly caterpillars stick themselves on to branches and stems with a pad of silk before pupating. Then they shed their old skin without dropping to the ground. Other caterpillars bury themselves in the soil or leaf litter.

▲ **HIBERNATING PUPA**
Some pupae, such as this Brown Hairstreak butterfly, complete their development in a couple of weeks. Other species pass the winter in a state of suspended development called diapause. This is very common among temperate butterflies and moths.

Pupa sticking upwards, held in place by a silk thread.

► **UP OR DOWN**
The pupae of White and Swallowtail butterflies stick upwards, held in place by a silk thread around the middle. These are called succinct pupae. Other pupae hang head-down from branches. They are called suspended pupae.

Elephant Hawk moth pupa with wing veins visible through the surface.

Old skin shed during the caterpillar's transformation into a pupa.

◄ DEVELOPING PUPA

The outlines of the wings, legs and antennae are faintly visible on the surface of the pupa showing that it is almost ready to hatch. Inside, the tissues that made up the caterpillar's body dissolve, ready for rebuilding as an adult.

FAILED PROTECTION ▶

The pupa of this Emperor moth (*Saturnia pavonia*) has been eaten away from the inside by the larva of a parasitic fly. The cocoon has been cut away to reveal the hole from which the fly grub has emerged. Pupae are never completely safe from predators.

Hole in moth pupa.

Pupa of parasite.

The Butterfly Lovers

An old Chinese tale tells of Zhu Yingtai, who disguises herself as a boy to go to college. There, she falls in love with Liang Shanbo. But Liang is unaware she is a girl and Zhu is forced to marry a rich man's son. Liang realises his mistake and dies broken-hearted. When Zhu hears, she takes her life in despair. The gods take pity and the pair are reunited as butterflies.

Did you know? Some pupae resemble dead leaves or even bird droppings to trick predators.

Moth just hatched from pupa in cocoon.

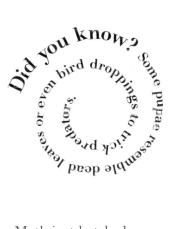

▶ EMERGING ADULT

Butterfly pupae vary considerably in colour and shape. Some Fritillary butterfly pupae have shiny patches that look like raindrops, but most moth pupae are brown or black bullet-shaped objects. Even experts find it difficult to tell the species to which they belong. Only when all the changes are complete and the moth emerges as an imago (adult) does the identity of the insect become clear.

Rear claspers grip a silken pad.

Focus on

Pupation (changing from a caterpillar to a butterfly or moth) is one of the most astonishing transformations undergone by any living creature. Inside the chrysalis, or pupa, the body parts of the caterpillar gradually dissolve. New features grow in their place, including a totally different head and body, and two pairs of wings. This whole process can take less than a week. When these changes are complete, a fully-formed imago (adult moth or butterfly) emerges almost magically from the nondescript pouch.

1 The Monarch butterfly caterpillar *(Danaus plexippus)* spins a silken pad on a plant stem and grips it firmly with its rear claspers. It then sheds its skin to reveal the chrysalis, which clings to the silken pad with tiny hooks.

2 The chrysalis of the Monarch is plump, pale and studded with golden spots. It appears lifeless except for the occasional twitch. However, changes can sometimes be vaguely seen through the skin.

Fully formed chrysalis.

Chrysalis darkens before opening.

3 The chrysalis grows dark just before the adult emerges. The wing pattern becomes visible through the skin. The butterfly then pumps body fluids to its head and thorax. Next, the chrysalis cracks open behind the head and along the front of the wing.

Metamorphosis

4 The butterfly swallows air to make itself swell up, which splits the chrysalis even more. The insect emerges shakily and hangs down, clinging tightly to the chrysalis skin.

Wings are soft and crumpled.

5 The newly emerged adult slowly pumps blood into the veins in its wings, which begin to straighten out. The insect hangs down with its head up so that the force of gravity helps to stretch the wings. After about half an hour, it reaches its full size.

Split skin of chrysalis

Wing veins with blood pumping into them.

6 The butterfly basks in the sun for an hour or two while its wings dry out and harden. After a few trial flaps of its wings, it is ready to fly away and begin its life as an adult butterfly.

The adult butterfly tests its wings before its maiden flight.

Finding a Mate

Common Blue butterfly
(Polyommatus icarus)

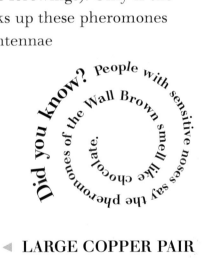

A butterfly's life is usually very short, so it has only a little while to find a mate. Most females live for just a few days, so they must begin to lay eggs as soon as possible. Male butterflies emerge from their pupae a little earlier than the females. This allows some males to mate with a newly emerged female while her wings are still soft and crumpled. However, most males court their female with elaborate flights and dances. Males and females are drawn to each other by the shape of each other's wings and by the colourful and striking patterns on them. The males also spread powerful scents that stimulate females to approach them and land alongside. Then they circle each other, performing complicated courtship dances.

▲ **COURTING BLUES**

When courting a female, a male butterfly often flutters its wings flamboyantly. It looks as if it is showing off, but it is really wafting its pheromones (the scents from special scales on its forewings). Only if the female picks up these pheromones with her antennae will she be willing to mate.

Did you know? People with sensitive noses say the pheromones of the Wall Brown smell like the chocolate.

◄ **LARGE COPPER PAIR**

This pair of butterflies is about to mate. When she is ready, the female will fly away and land with her wings half open. The male will flutter down on top of her and begin to caress her abdomen with his rear end. The male then turns around to face the opposite way as they couple. The pair may remain joined like this for hours.

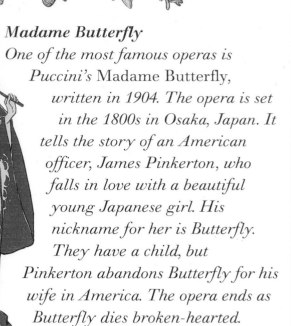

Madame Butterfly
One of the most famous operas is
Puccini's Madame Butterfly,
written in 1904. The opera is set
in the 1800s in Osaka, Japan. It
tells the story of an American
officer, James Pinkerton, who
falls in love with a beautiful
young Japanese girl. His
nickname for her is Butterfly.
They have a child, but
Pinkerton abandons Butterfly for his
wife in America. The opera ends as
Butterfly dies broken-hearted.

▼ SCENT POWER

A butterfly's scent plays a major role in attracting a mate. The scents come from glands on the abdomen of a female. On a male, the scents come from special wing scales called androconia. A male often rubs his wings over the female's antennae.

Androconia scales
release scent.

▼ MALE AND FEMALE

Often, female butterflies are drab, while males are brightly coloured. The male Orange-tip, for example, has a distinctive bright orange coloured tip to its wings. However, the ends of the female Orange-tip's wings (see top right of page) are grey-black.

Male Orange-tip butterfly *(Anthocharis cardamines)*

▼ SINGLE MATE

Male butterflies mate several times in their lifetime. However a female butterfly usually mates just once and then concentrates on egg-laying. Once they have mated, many females release a special pheromone that deters other males.

Female Orange-tip butterfly *(Anthocharis cardamines)*

▲ FLYING TOGETHER

Butterflies usually stay on the ground or on a plant while coupling. But if danger threatens, they can fly off linked together, with one (called the carrier) pulling the other backwards.

Flower Power

Butterflies and moths have a close relationship with plants, especially with those that flower. Many live much of their lives on a particular kind of vegetation. They begin life as eggs on the plant, feed on it while they are caterpillars and change into a pupa while attached to it. Finally the adult may sip the nectar from its blooms. Just as butterflies rely on flowers for food, many flowers rely on visiting butterflies to spread their pollen. The bright colours and attractive scents of flowers may have evolved to attract butterflies and other insects such as bees. When a butterfly lands on a flower to drink nectar, grains of pollen cling to its body. Some of the pollen grains rub off on the next bloom the butterfly visits.

▲ FEEDING ON FUCHSIA

The caterpillar of the Elephant Hawk moth feeds on the leaves of fuchsia. Many lepidopterists (butterfly and moth experts) grow fuchsias in their gardens for the pleasure of seeing this spectacular caterpillar. However, some gardeners think of the moths as pests for the same reason.

▼ THISTLE LOVER

A Brimstone butterfly (*Gonepteryx rhamni*) settles on a thistle to feed. It is common throughout Europe in light woodland and in open countryside at heights of up to 2000m. The Brimstone also likes to feed on a wide range of garden flowers.

▲ FABULOUS FUCHSIAS

The Small Elephant Hawk moth is shown here drinking nectar from a fuchsia. Rather than settling on a flower, these large, powerful moths often feed while hovering in front of them.

▶ FEEDING TOGETHER

A group of Small Tortoiseshell butterflies (*Aglais urticae*) are shown here sipping nectar together. Small Tortoiseshells are widespread throughout Europe. They are attracted to a wide range of blooms including buddleia, Michaelmas daisy and sedum that are found in fields, by roadsides and in back gardens.

◀ STINGING NETTLES

The adult Peacock butterfly (*Inachis io*) sits on a weed called the stinging nettle. It generally feeds on flowers such as buddleia. However, the caterpillars of this species feed almost exclusively on nettles. Many gardeners clear away this unattractive weed, which causes Peacock butterflies to lay their eggs elsewhere.

Did you know? Buddleia is so attractive to many butterflies that it is sometimes called the butterfly bush.

▼ GOURMET FOOD

This beautiful Red Spotted Purple Swallowtail feeds on a desert flower in Arizona, North America. Butterflies and moths are adapted to the specific environment in which they live. Swallowtails are common throughout Europe but there they sip nectar from meadow and orchard flowers.

Red Spotted Purple Swallowtail butterfly (*Basilarchia astyanax*)

33

Nectar and Food

Postman butterfly
(*Heliconius*)

Butterflies and moths cannot chew food. Instead, they suck up liquids through their long proboscises (tongues), which act like drinking straws. Their preferred food is nectar. This sugary fluid is produced in the nectaries of flowers in order to attract insects such as butterflies and bees. Most species of butterfly survive on nectar alone and spend most of their brief lives flitting from flower to flower in search of this juice. Some woodland species extract sweet liquids from a wide variety of sources, including rotting fruit and sap oozing from wounds in trees. A few species even suck on dung. However, these sources do not provide much real sustenance, which is why butterflies rarely live for more than a few days.

▲ LONG LIFE

Heliconius butterflies of the tropical forests of South America are among the few relatively long-lived butterflies. They are able to live for 130 days or more, compared with barely 20 for most temperate species. *Heliconius* butterflies feed on passionfruit flowers.

Red Admiral butterfly
(*Vanessa atalanta*)

▼ CIDER DRINKING

In autumn, butterflies such as the Red Admiral and the Camberwell Beauty often feed on rotting fruit. Sometimes the juice has fermented to alcohol, and the Red Admiral may be seen reeling around as if drunk.

▲ FRUIT EATERS

The first generation of Comma butterflies appears each year in early summer. These insects feed on the delicate white blossoms of brambles (blackberries), because the fruit has not ripened at this time. The second generation appear in autumn, so they feed on the ripe blackberry fruits.

◄ DRINKING STRAW

Many flowers hide their nectaries deep inside the blooms in order to draw the butterfly right on to their pollen sacs. Many butterflies have developed very long proboscises to reach the nectar. They probe deep into the flower to suck up the juice.

Did you know? The Purple Emperor butterfly often survives by sucking juices from the rotting bodies of dead animals.

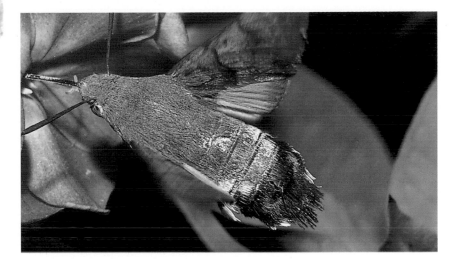

▲ HOVERING HAWK MOTHS

The day-flying Hummingbird Hawk moth gets its name from its habit of hovering in front of flowers like a hummingbird as it sips nectar, rather than landing on the flower. The hawk moth family have the longest proboscises of all. One member, known as Darwin's Hawk moth, has a proboscis that reaches to between 30 and 35cm – about three times the length of its body.

► WOODLAND VARIETY

Many woodland butterflies extract juices from a variety of sources. The Speckled Wood butterfly sometimes sips nectar from bluebells. However, it feeds mainly on honeydew. This is the sugary secretion of tiny insects called aphids. The leaves of flowers are often coated with honeydew.

▲ NIGHT FEEDER

Noctuid moths often sip nectar from ragworts in meadows by moonlight. In temperate countries, these moths mostly feed on warm summer nights. They get their name from the Latin word *noctuis*, which means night.

Speckled Wood butterfly
(Pararge aegeria)

35

At Ground Level

Butterflies need warmth in order to fly. In tropical regions it is usually warm enough for butterflies to fly for most of the day. But in cooler countries, they often spend much of the day resting. They spread out their wings and turn with the sun to soak up the rays. Male butterflies and moths also gather at muddy puddles or on damp earth to drink. This activity is known as puddling. At dusk, most butterflies seek a safe place to roost (rest) for the night. Moths generally hide themselves away during the day. They conceal themselves against tree bark or under leaves so they cannot be seen by predators.

▲ LAZY DAYS

A day's undisturbed rest is important for night-flying moths such as this Sussex Emerald. It rests on or under leaves with its green wings outstretched, well disguised amongst the vegetation. Most other Geometer moths rest in this position during the day too, on leaves or against tree bark. Before flight, they shiver to warm up their wings.

▲ DRY PUDDLING

A Malayan butterfly sucks up mineral-rich water from sand through its proboscis (tongue). Some species of butterfly do not need a puddle in order to go puddling. In some dry regions, the male butterfly may be able to get the sodium salts it needs by spitting on and sucking dry stones, gravel or even the dried carcasses of animals.

▲ SALT SEEKERS

Puddling is a common activity in warm regions. However it is not a communal activity. In some regions butterflies and moths puddle on their own. Although they appear to be drinking, only males seem to puddle like this. It is believed that they absorb important salts dissolved in the water. Sodium salts are needed to produce the sperm packets passed on to females during mating.

► **BASKING ON LICHEN**
A Small Tortoiseshell butterfly (*Aglais urticae*) basks in a park on a carpet of lichen. It rests with its wings open wide and flat, to soak up the sun's warmth. The Small Tortoiseshell lives in cooler parts of the world, in Europe, Siberia and Japan. It therefore needs to bask in the sunshine to warm up its wing muscles before flight.

Did you know? The Grayling butterfly tilts to one side while resting to reduce the shadow cast by its wings.

▲ **SUN LOVERS**
The Marbled White and other members of the Satyridae family have an unusual way of holding their wings when basking. They are held in a V-shape instead of fully opened or folded upright. The white of their wings reflects sunlight on to their abdomens.

Black-veined White butterfly
(*Aporia crataegi*)

▲ **ROOSTING IN THE RAIN**
Most butterflies escape the worst of the rain by roosting under leaves, but some of them stay out in the open. With their wings tightly closed, like this Black-veined White, the rain just runs over their scales and drips off. The wings dry almost immediately when the sun comes out.

Focus on

Skippers are not closely related to other butterflies. Most are less than 40mm across, with swept-back wings that make them highly agile. Skippers beat their wings rapidly and can change direction suddenly in mid-air, quite unlike other butterflies. The name Skipper refers to this darting, dancing flight. More than 3,000 species exist worldwide, including about 40 in Europe and 300 or more in North America. Most Skippers are brown or orange, but some tropical species, such as the Peruvian Skipper, have brilliant colours.

SHAPES
The body of this rainforest butterfly (*Haemactis sanguinalis*) is typical of all Skippers. It has a plump, hairy body that is more like a moth's than a butterfly's. The tips of their antennae are hooked not clubbed like other butterflies.

CIGAR CATERPILLARS
Skipper caterpillars are shaped like smooth cigars. They have distinct necks and their heads are usually different in colour from the rest of their bodies. They normally live in shelters made of leaves and spun silk.

Skippers

NIGHT-FLYING SKIPPER

This Peruvian Skipper is not as drab and moth-like as many Skippers but, like moths, it flies at night. It flies with a whirring sound produced by its wing beats. This is another feature Skippers share with moths.

TRINIDAD SKIPPERS

Most skippers in Europe and North America are dull shades of brown and many resemble moths more than butterflies. However, many tropical species are more brightly coloured, including this pair from Trinidad in the West Indies.

THISTLE FEEDER

The Silver-spotted Skipper haunts chalk hills and flies close to the ground. It likes to roost and feed on the flowers of low-growing thistles. Although it basks like the Large Skipper (*right*), it shuts its wings in dull weather.

GOLDEN SKIPPERS

The Large Skipper, seen here on knapweed, is a member of a group called Golden Skippers. They bask in an unusual way, flattening their hindwings and tilting their forewings forward. Male Golden Skippers have scent scales in a black streak in the middle of their wing.

Migration

Some butterflies and moths live and die within a very small area, never moving far from their birthplace. However, a few species are regular migrants. They are able to travel astonishing distances in search of new plant growth, or to escape cold or overpopulated areas. Some butterflies are truly worldwide migrants in a similar way to migratory birds. Every now and then small swarms of North American butterflies turn up in Europe after crossing the Atlantic Ocean. Crimson-speckled moths have been spotted thousands of kilometres out over the Southern Atlantic. Nevertheless, butterflies are unlike birds in that most only migrate one way and do not return to their original homes.

Canada

Atlantic Ocean

Pacific
Ocean

USA

Mexico

Central
America

Migration path

▲ **MONARCH ROUTES**
Monarch butterflies (*Danaus plexippus*) migrate mainly between North and Central America. A few have crossed the Atlantic and settled on islands off Africa and Portugal. Others have flown all the way to Ireland.

▲ **MONARCH MASSES**
Every autumn huge numbers of Monarchs leave eastern and western North America and fly south. They spend the winter in Florida, California and Mexico on the same trees settled by their grandparents the previous year.

▲ **KING OF MIGRANTS**
In March, Monarch butterflies journey over 3000km northwards, lay their eggs on the way and die. When the eggs hatch the cycle begins again. The month-old butterflies either continue north or return south, depending on the season.

◄ AN AFRICAN MIGRANT

This Brown veined White butterfly has large wings capable of carrying it over long distances. Millions of these butterflies form swarms in many parts of southern Africa. A swarm can cause chaos to people attempting to drive through it. Although this butterfly flies throughout the year, these swarms are seen most often in December and January.

Did you know? A large swarm of migrating butterflies can bring farm machines to a standstill by resting on them.

► HAWK MOTH

Every spring thousands of Oleander Hawk moths set off from their native tropical Africa and head north. A few of them reach the far north of Europe in late summer. Hawk moths are among the furthest flying of all moths. They are able to travel rapidly over long distances.

Oleander Hawk moth *(Daphnis nerii)*

▲ HIBERNATING PEACOCK

The adult Peacock butterfly sleeps during the winter. This sleep is called hibernation. The Peacock is protected by chemicals called glycols that stop its body fluids from freezing. Many other butterflies and moths survive the winter in this way instead of migrating.

► PAINTED LADY

The Painted Lady butterfly *(Vanessa cardui)* migrates almost all over the world. In summer it is found across Europe, as far as north as Iceland. However, it cannot survive the winter frosts. Adults emerging in late summer head south, and a few reach North Africa before the autumn chill starts.

41

Enemies and Disease

Many butterflies and moths lay huge numbers of eggs. Sometimes a single female can lay more than a thousand at any one time. However, these eggs are attacked by predators, parasites and disease from the moment they are laid. Caterpillars and adults also have many enemies and are preyed on by creatures such as birds, bats, lizards, spiders, hornets, and beetles. They are also attacked by parasitic wasps and flies that lay eggs inside caterpillars' bodies. Those that survive the attack of these predators and parasites may fall victim to diseases or harmful fungi.

▲ DEADLY BIRDS

Birds are the most dangerous enemies of butterflies and moths. Many types of bird prey upon adult insects. In spring, birds such as blue tits are often seen flying back to their nests with beakfuls of fat, juicy caterpillars for their young.

▲ BAT ATTACK

An Eyed Hawk moth is devoured by a Serotine Bat, leaving only wings and eggs. Night-flying moths often fall victim to bats, who can track them down in pitch darkness.

▲ PROWLING FOXES

Foxes seem unlikely predators of caterpillars. Surprisingly, though, when scientists have examined the stomach contents of dead foxes, they have found huge quantities of caterpillars. Foxes are sometimes forced to eat caterpillars when other food is scarce.

▶ UNWELCOME GUESTS

An Eyed Hawk moth caterpillar is killed by parasitic flies of the Tachinidae family. Many caterpillars are killed in this way. The fly injects its eggs into the caterpillar's body, and the newly hatched grubs eat away the body from the inside. The grubs grow and eventually bore their way out.

Gatekeeper butterfly
(*Pyronia tithonus*)

Clump of red mites.

◀ RED MITES

The red blob on the back of this Gatekeeper butterfly is a clump of red mites. These mites are larvae that cling on to butterflies of the Satyridae family. They feed on the butterfly's blood until they are full and then drop off, apparently doing the butterfly little harm.

▶ POUNCING SPIDERS

A butterfly that is sitting motionless on a flower for a long time may not be resting. It may have been killed by a crab spider. Creamy yellow crab spiders blend in so well on flower heads that many butterflies do not notice them and fall victim to their deadly venom.

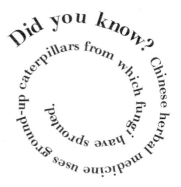

Crab spider with its fangs in an unsuspecting victim.

European Map butterfly
(*Araschnia levana*)

Did you know? Chinese herbal medicine uses ground-up caterpillars from which fungi have sprouted.

A Citrus Swallowtail pupa mimics a curled-up green leaf. Pupae remain motionless for weeks and are highly vulnerable, so camouflage is often their only protection.

Citrus Swallowtail butterfly pupa (Papilio demodocus)

Camouflage

Caterpillars and adult butterflies and moths are so vulnerable to attack that many have become masters of disguise. They hide from prying eyes by taking on the colours of trees, leaves and rocks. This defence is known as camouflage. Many moths fold back their wings during the day so they look like a leaf or a piece of bark. Most caterpillars are green to mimic leaves and grass or brown to mimic bark and mud. Inchworms (the caterpillars of Looper moths) are coloured and shaped to look just like twigs and even cling to stems at a twiglike angle.

Did you know? Emperor moth caterpillars blend in with heather leaves when small and heather stems when they grow larger.

▼ **LEAF MIMIC**

A wing of the Brazilian butterfly *Zaretis itis* looks like a dead leaf. The wing even mimics a leaf's natural tears and the spots made on it by fungi.

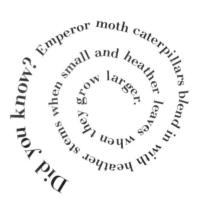

Zaretis itis

▲ **LYING LOW**

Geometrid moths are not easy to spot amongst dead leaves on the floor of a rainforest in Costa Rica. Another Costa Rican moth disguises itself as lichen. Moths rest in broad daylight, so they need to be especially well camouflaged.

▲ HIDDEN LARVA

The caterpillar of the Orchard Swallowtail is camouflaged as a bird-dropping. Other caterpillars are brown or green, so they blend in with vegetation.

▲ FOLIAGE FRIENDLY

A Brimstone butterfly camouflages itself as a leaf by folding up its wings so that only the green underside is visible. The upper side of this butterfly's wings are the colour of brimstone (bright yellow), which is how the insect got its name.

Did you know? The moth Belenoptera sanguine rests with the front of its wings rolled up to resemble a leaf stalk.

▲ PINE MIMIC

The Pine Hawk moth (*Hyloicus pinastri*) is perfectly adapted to the pine forests in which it lives. Its mottled silvery-grey wings match the bark of pine trees. The moth is almost impossible to spot when it roosts during the day. Other moths imitate the bark of different trees.

▶ TWIGS

The Peppered moth caterpillar resembles a twig. It even has warts on its body like the buds on a twig. In the 1800s, a darker form of the adult moth became more common. This was because the soot from factories made tree trunks sooty. The darker moth blended in better on the dark trunks.

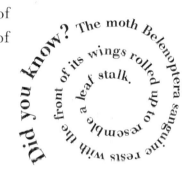

Peppered moth caterpillar
(*Biston betularia*)

45

Spotted Tiger moth
(Rhypasia purpurava)

Decoys and Displays

Camouflage helps to keep resting moths and butterflies hidden from the eyes of predators, but as soon as they move they become visible. Therefore butterflies and moths that fly during daylight hours must adopt other strategies to escape. The upper wings of many butterflies are coloured in all kinds of surprising ways to fool predators. Some mimic dangerous creatures. For example, the striped body, transparent wings and buzzing flight of a Hornet Clearwing moth make it resemble a stinging wasp from a distance. Others use colours or their wing shapes to confuse their predators. False antennae and eyes fool them into attacking from the wrong direction.

▲ CONFUSION

A Spotted Tiger moth escapes predators by surprising them with a quick flash of its brightly coloured underwings. When the moth is resting, these wings are hidden beneath its yellow forewings. A sudden flash of colour is often enough to confuse an enemy.

▶ BIG EYES

A Japanese Owl moth (*Brahmaea japonica*) flashes giant spots at a foe when threatened. These spots look like the staring eyes of a big owl, which scares off birds, lizards and other predators. Other moths display bright parts of their wings while in flight. When they are being chased, the predator focuses on the moth's bright wing. However, as soon as the moth lands the colour is hidden and the predator is confused.

▲ TRICK OF THE EYE

Eyed Hawk moths have big eye spots on their hindwings. When in danger, the moth startles its enemy by flinging its wings open to reveal the enormous false eyes beneath.

Eye spots are hidden by forewings.

▶ SHUT EYES

A mating pair of Eyed Hawk moths hide their eye spots beneath their forewings. The effectiveness of eye spots depends on flashing them suddenly. To an inquisitive predator, it looks just like a cat or an owl opening its eyes – and the bird is frightened away.

Did you know? Some moth pupae produce squeaks to deter predators from eating them.

▶ TWO HEADS ARE BETTER THAN ONE...

This blue butterfly's secret escape system is the false eyes and mock antennae on its rear end. Predatory birds are fooled into lunging for the flimsy false head rather than the butterfly's real head at the other end. The butterfly then slips away from the bird's beak.

False eyes and antennae.

▲ WASP IMPERSONATOR

The Hornet Clearwing moth loses most of the scales from its wings on its first flight and then looks just like a wasp. Birds fear it has a vicious sting, although it is harmless.

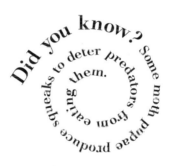

▼ DECOY EYES

A Little Wood Satyr has false eyes at the edges of its wings. A huge number of butterflies and moths have similar spots on their wings. Birds peck at them, thinking they are real eyes. Butterflies are often seen flying with pieces bitten out of their wing edges. They do not seem to be troubled by having parts of their wings missing and are able to fly as normal.

Chemical Weapons

African Euchromia moth (*Euchromia lethe*)

Most butterflies and moths escape their enemies by avoiding being spotted. However, some use other tricks. They cannot sting or bite like bees or wasps, but many caterpillars have different ways of using toxic chemicals to poison their attackers, or at least make themselves unpleasant to taste or smell. For example, the caterpillar of the Brown-tail moth has barbed hairs tipped with a poison that can cause a severe skin rash even in humans. A Cinnabar moth cannot poison a predator, but it tastes foul if eaten. Usually, caterpillars that are unpalatable to predators are brightly coloured to let potential attackers know that they should be avoided.

▲ **BRIGHT AND DEADLY**

The brilliant colours of the African Euchromia moth warn any would-be predators that it is poisonous. It also has an awful smell. Some moths manufacture their own poisons, but others are toxic because their caterpillars eat poisonous plants. The poisons do not hurt the insects, but make them harmful to their enemies.

▲ **HAIRY MOUTHFUL**

The caterpillar of the Sycamore moth (*Apatele aceris*) is bright yellow. It is poisonous like some other brightly coloured caterpillars, but its masses of long, hairy tufts make it distinctly unpleasant to eat.

▼ **THREATENING DISPLAY**

The caterpillar of the Puss Moth may look as brightly coloured as a clown, but by caterpillar standards it is quite fearsome. When threatened, its slender whip-like tails are thrust forwards and it may squirt a jet of harmful formic acid from a gland near its mouth. It also uses red markings and false eye spots on its head to create an aggressive display.

Whip-like tail to threaten predators.

Puss Moth caterpillar (*Cerura vinula*)

◄ POISON MILK

A Monarch butterfly caterpillar feeds on various kinds of milkweed which contain a powerful poison. This chemical is harmful to many small creatures. The poison stays in the Monarch's body throughout its life. This may be why Monarchs show less fear of predators than other butterflies.

► RED ALERT

The striking red, white and black colours of the Spurge Hawk moth caterpillar announce that it is poisonous. Unpalatable insects frequently display conspicuous colours such as reds, yellows, blacks and white. These insects do not need to protect themselves by blending into their background. This caterpillar acquires its poison from a plant called spurge.

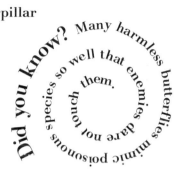

Spurge Hawk moth caterpillar
(Hyles euphorbiae)

Did you know? Many harmless butterflies mimic poisonous species so well that enemies dare not touch them.

▼ SMELLY CATERPILLARS

The Swallowtail caterpillar produces an odour that is strong enough to ward off parasites. It comes from a scent-gland called the osmeterium situated just behind its head. This gland suddenly erupts and oozes acid when the caterpillar is threatened.

▲ DEFENSIVE FROTH

Rhodogastria moths of Australasia often have a bright red abdomen to warn others that they carry a deadly poison. When the moth is threatened, this poison oozes as a green froth from a gland on the back of its neck.

Swallowtail caterpillar
(Papilio machaon)

Around the World

Butterflies and moths are surprisingly adaptable creatures. Almost every land mass in the world has its own particular range of butterfly and moth species. They inhabit a huge variety of different places, from the fringes of the hottest deserts to the icy wastes of the Arctic. Species are adapted to living in these very different environments. For example, butterflies and moths that live in cold areas tend to be darker than those that live in warm regions. This is because they need to be warm in order to fly and dark colours soak up sunlight more easily. In mountainous areas, the local species usually fly close to the ground. Flying any higher than this would create a risk of being blown away by the strong winds.

Orange-tip butterfly
(Anthocharis cardamines)

◄ MEADOWS AND WAYSIDES

Farmland is an increasingly hostile habitat for butterflies. Intensive cultivation strips away wild flowers and grasses, while crop-spraying poisons the insects. However, many butterflies still thrive in meadows and hedgerows around the fields. Orange-tips, Meadow Browns, Gatekeepers, Small Coppers, Whites and Blues are still common, as are Noctuid and Geometrid moths.

Apollo butterfly
(Parnassius apollo)

◄ MOUNTAINS

Butterflies that are adapted to life high on the mountains include the Alpine and Mountain Arguses and the Apollo. The Apollo's body is covered with fur to protect it from the extreme cold. Most Apollo eggs that are laid in autumn do not hatch until the following spring because of the low temperatures. Those caterpillars that do hatch hibernate at once.

◄ MARSHES AND WETLANDS

The Marsh Fritillary flourishes among the grasses and flowers of wetlands in temperate regions (areas that have warm summers and cold winters). Its caterpillar's favourite food plant is devil's bit scabious. Among the many other butterflies that thrive in wetlands are the Swallowtail, the White Peacock, and the Painted Skipper.

▶ DIFFERENT HABITATS

Butterflies and moths inhabit a wide range of regions. Species such as the Large White live in town gardens, while Graylings, Spanish Festoons and Two-tailed Pashas often live in coastal areas. Deserts are home to Painted Ladies, and White Admirals flutter about in woodland glades. Arctic species include the Pale Arctic and Clouded Yellow. Apollos and Cynthia's Fritillary are examples of Alpine types.

▼ GARDENS

All kinds of butterflies and moths visit gardens, including the Peacock (*Inachis io*). Here they find an abundance of flowers to feed on – not only weeds, but also many garden flowers. Many of these flowers are actually related to wild hedgerow and field flowers such as buddleias, aubretias and Michaelmas daisies.

The Warrior Symbol

A statue of a proud warrior stands at the ancient Toltec capital city of Tula in Mexico. An image of a butterfly appears on the warrior's breastplate. The Toltec people knew that butterflies live short but brilliant lives. Consequently, the butterfly became a symbol for Toltec soldiers who lived a brave life and did not fear death.

Indian Moon moth
(Actias selene)

Tropical Species

More species of butterfly and moth live in tropical parts of the world (regions near the Equator) than anywhere else. Tens of thousands of known species populate the tropical rainforests, and new species are being discovered almost every day. Some of the most spectacular and beautiful of all butterflies live in the tropics. These include shimmering Blue Morphos, vivid Orange Albatrosses, and exquisite Banded King Shoemakers. A large number of striking moths live in these areas, too, including the Indian and African Moon moths and the Golden Emperor.

▲ **MOONLIT MOTH**

The ghostly green-white wings of the Moon moth shine dimly on moonlit nights in forests ranging from Indonesia to India. Its huge wings measure 12cm in width and up to 18cm in length. The long tails, which are shaped like crescent moons, flutter in the shadows beneath the trees.

Painted Lady
(Vanessa cardui)

▲ **POSTMAN BUTTERFLY**

The brightly coloured Postman butterfly is found across a wide area of South America and has many different sub-species. These butterflies eat pollen as well as nectar.

▲ **DESERT WANDERER**

The Painted Lady butterfly lives in warm regions, although in summer it is often seen far to the north in Europe and North America. In autumn, it flies south to avoid perishing in the cold. In Africa, the natural homes of this species are the edges of the Sahara desert.

▶ EMERALD JEWEL

The Swallowtail family of butterflies (known by
scientists as the Papilionids) includes some of the
biggest and most beautiful of all butterflies. Among
the most prized is the shimmering green
Papilio palinurus that lives in the
rainforests of South-east Asia.
Its green colouring blends in
perfectly with the lush
vegetation. Many types of
Swallowtail are protected
species because of humans
cutting down large areas of rainforest.

Green Swallowtail butterfly
(Papilio palinurus)

◀ METALMARK

A Metalmark (*Caria mantinea*) feeds on salts
from damp ground. This butterfly is one of
the Metalmark (or Riodinidae) family. It is
one of the few families that are almost
entirely restricted to the tropics. Their
distinctive, rapid zigzag flight is often
seen in rainforests.

▶ WISE OWL

Owl butterflies, such as *Caligo
memnon* of South and Central
America, are some of the most
distinctive of all tropical
butterflies. Their large eyespots
suggest the staring eyes of an owl.
They feed mainly on bananas. For
this reason, many owners of
banana plantations regard these
butterflies as pests.

Did you know? The Cattle Heart Swallowtail of Central and South America flies at heights of up to 1,500m along the edges of rainforests.

Owl butterfly
(Caligo memnon)

Woodland Species

Purple hairstreak
(Quercusia quercus)

Butterflies and moths have suffered from intensive farming in open country, but they still flourish in woodlands. A small number live in dense woods where there are few flowers. Larger numbers gather around clearings or glades. Certain species live mostly at low, shady levels while others prefer to dwell high among the treetops. The largest number of species live in mixed woodland, where food sources are varied. However, some species prefer particular kinds of woodland. For example, the Pine Hawk moth is common in coniferous forests, the Lobster moth is found in beech woods and the Green Oak Tortrix likes oak woodlands.

▲ OAK EATER
The Purple Hairstreak's favoured food plant is the oak tree. It can be found almost anywhere where large oaks grow in Africa and Asia. The adults do not seek out flowers for nectar because they flutter high in trees to feed on honeydew (a sweet liquid secreted by aphids).

▲ SHIMMERING PURPLE
The Lesser Purple Emperor *(Apatura ilia)* and its cousin the Purple Emperor are among the most magnificent of all woodland butterflies. Their rapid, soaring flight is highly distinctive, as are their shimmering purple wings. They can often be seen near streams and ponds around willows, on which their caterpillars feed.

▲ DEAD LEAF MOTH
The Lappet moth is perfectly adapted to woodland life. When its wings are folded in rest it looks just like a dead leaf. Its caterpillar feeds on blackthorn, apple and other fruit trees, and is regarded as a pest by orchard owners.

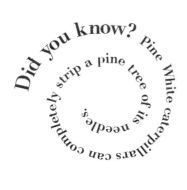
▶ FRITILLARY FLUTTER

The Silver-washed Fritillary is one of a large number of related species that inhabit woodlands. It can often be seen gliding through clearings and over woodland paths searching for nectar-rich bramble blossom. Its caterpillars feed on violet leaves.

Silver-washed Fritillary
(*Argynnis paphia*)

◀ OAK MOTH

The Oak Hooktip moth (*Drepana binaria*) lives in woodlands wherever there are oak trees. It flies mainly at night, but is sometimes seen on sunny afternoons. Its browny colouring blends perfectly with the bark on which it rests. Its caterpillar feeds on oak leaves. When it is fully grown it pupates inside a cocoon spun between two oak leaves.

The Legend of Etain
An old Irish myth tells of Etain, who became a butterfly. At first, he was changed into a puddle by his first wife, who was jealous when he remarried. A worm was born from the puddle. This turned into a beautiful butterfly which was sheltered and guarded by the gods.

▲ SPOTS AND STREAKS

The Brindled Beauty gets its name from the feathery bands on its wings. The word brindled means marked with spots or streaks. As well as living in woods, it is common in parks and gardens. Its caterpillars eat the leaves of various trees.

Focus on

1 Hawk moths begin life as eggs laid on the leaves of the food-plant. The round eggs are a distinctive shiny green. They are laid singly or in small batches and hatch a week or two afterwards.

2 The Elephant Hawk moth's name comes from the ability of its caterpillar to stretch out its front segments like an elephant's trunk. It takes about six weeks to grow fully and, like most hawk moths, it passes the winter in the pupal stage.

Hawk moths are perhaps the most distinctive of all the moth families. Their scientific name is *Sphingidae*. Their bodies are unusually large and they are strong fliers. Hawk moths can fly at speeds of up to 50km an hour, and many hover like a hummingbird while feeding from flowers. Many hawk moths have very long tongues that enable them to sip nectar from even the deepest flowers. When these moths come to rest, their wings usually angle back like the wings of a jet plane. Hawk moth caterpillars nearly all have a pointed horn on the end of their bodies.

3 The adult Elephant Hawk moth is one of the prettiest of all moths. It flies for a few weeks in the summer. Its candy-pink wings are a perfect match for the pink garden fuchsias and wild willow-herbs on which it lays its eggs.

Hawk Moths

POPLAR HAWK MOTHS

During the late spring and summer, Poplar hawk moths can often be seen flying towards lighted shop windows in European towns at night. They have a short tongue and do not feed. Unusually for hawk moths, when they are resting during the day, their hindwings are pushed in front of the forewings.

Poplar hawk moth
(Laothoe populi)

HONEY LOVER

The Death's Head Hawk moth (*Acherontia atropos*) is named after the skull-like markings near the back of its head. Its proboscis is too short to sip nectar. Instead, it sometimes enters beehives and sucks honey from the combs.

MASTER OF DISGUISE

The Broad-bordered Bee Hawk moth (*Hemaris fuciformis*) resembles a bumblebee. It has a fat, brown and yellow body and clear, glassy wings. This helps protect it from predators as it flies during the day.

Superfamilies

Scientists group butterflies and moths into 24 groups known as superfamilies. All but two of these superfamilies are moths, ranging from the tiny Micropterigoidea to the huge Bombycoidea. This latter group contains the giant Atlas moths. Butterflies belong to the other two superfamilies. The first, Hesperoidea, includes all 3,000 or so species of Skippers. The second, Papilionoidea, consists of about 15,000 species, divided among several families. These families include Papilionidae (Swallowtails, Apollos and Festoons), Pieridae (Whites and Yellows), Lycaenidae (Blues, Coppers and Hairstreaks) and Nymphalidae (Fritillaries, Morphos, Monarchs, Browns and Satyrs).

▲ **FEATHERY FAMILY**
The Plume moths (Pterophoridae) are small but very distinctive. They get their name from the way their wings are branched in feathery fronds, making them look almost like craneflies.

European Swallowtail butterfly (*Papilio machaon*)

Garden Tiger moth (*Arctia caja*)

◄ **ARCTIIDAE**
Tiger moths belong to a family of moths called the Arctiidae. Many of them are protected from predators by highly distasteful body fluids and a coat of irritating hairs, which they announce with their striking colours and bold patterns.

▲ **GREAT BEAUTIES**
Swallowtail butterflies belong to a family called Papilionidae. This family contains about 600 species. It includes some of the largest and most beautiful of all butterflies, such as the Birdwings of South-east Asia and the African Giant Swallowtail, whose large wings reach about 25cm across.

◄ THE BRUSH-FOOTS

The Fritillaries belong to one of the largest families of butterflies, called the Nymphalidae. This family is sometimes known as the brush-foots, because their front legs are short and covered in tufts of hair. The Fritillaries get their name from *fritillaria*, the ancient Roman game of chequers.

▼ AN EXCLUSIVE BUNCH

The Japanese Oak Silk moth has brown wing markings, unlike the famous white Silk moth of China. Silk moths belong to a family of moths called the Bombycidae. Only 300 species of Bombycidae are known to exist. Silk moths are among the best known of all moths because of the ability of their caterpillars to spin large quantities of silk.

Japanese Oak Silk moth
(Antheraea pernyi)

This moth possesses distinctive clear windows in its wings.

▲ TROPICAL RELATIVES

The beautiful and aptly named Glasswing butterfly of South America is a member of a group called the Ithomiids. This group forms part of the larger Nymphalidae (or brush-foot) family, which are found all over the world. Ithomiids, however, live only in the tropics.

► SMALL WONDERS

The Longhorn moths belong to a family of tiny moths called the Incurvariidae. These European moths are often metallic in colour. Longhorn moths are easily recognised by their unusually long antennae.

59

Conservation

Ever-increasing numbers of butterfly and moth species are becoming rare or even endangered. Their homes are lost when forests are cut down, hedgerows pulled up, wetlands drained and fields sprayed with pesticides. All wild creatures have been endangered to some extent by human activity, but butterflies and moths have suffered more than most. The life of each species is dependent on a particular range of food plants. Any change in the habitat that damages food plants can threaten butterflies and moths. For example, the ploughing up of natural grassland has significantly reduced the numbers of Regal Fritillary in North America, while tourism in mountain areas may kill off the magnificent Apollo butterfly.

▲ **MORPHO JEWELLERY**
Millions of brilliant Blue Morpho butterflies are collected and made into jewellery. Only the brightly coloured males are collected, leaving the less colourful females to lay their eggs.

▼ **AT RISK**
The False Ringlet is probably Europe's most endangered butterfly. The drainage of its damp grassland habitats has led to its disappearance from all but a few areas.

False Ringlet
(Coenonympha oedippus)

▲ **FATAL COLLECTIONS?**
In the 1800s, millions of butterflies were caught and killed by collectors. However, their activities had little effect on populations, because each adult female lays more than enough eggs to make up the difference. However, the destruction of their habitats in the 1900s has now made some species so rare that collecting even a few specimens may tip the balance against their survival.

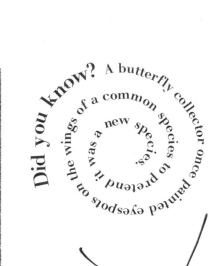

▼ PRIZED SWALLOWTAIL

The stunning Scarlet Swallowtail butterfly is found only in the Philippines. It is now under threat as its rainforest habitat is destroyed by urban development. Thoughtless collectors also trap this insect as a highly prized specimen.

▲ SLASH AND BURN

Rainforests are burned away by developers to create new farmland and towns. Many species of butterfly and moth are threatened by the destruction of their habitat.

Scarlet Swallowtail butterfly
(*Papilio rumanzovia*)

▲ PUSHED OUT

The Kentish Glory (*Endromis versicolora*) moth became extinct in England in the 1960s. This was when the birchwoods in which it lived were destroyed.

ANCIENT MEXICO

The ancient civilizations of Mexico were fascinated by the many brilliant butterflies that inhabit this part of the world. The people of Teotihuacan (around 150BC — AD650) adorned some of their temples with butterfly carvings. The Aztecs (around AD1200 — 1525) also worshipped a butterfly god.

GLOSSARY

abdomen
The abdomen is the rear section of the three parts of an insect's body. It holds the digestive system and the sex organs. In many female insects, it includes the ovipositor which is used to inject eggs.

androconia
Androconia are the special scales on a male butterfly's wings that release scent to attract females.

antenna
The plural of antenna is antennae. Antennae are the two feelers on an insect's head. They are the insect's most important sense receptors. Not only do they smell food, but they hear and feel things, too. Some antennae may even pick up taste and changes in temperature.

basal region
The basal region is the part of a butterfly's wing that lies closest to its body.

caterpillar
The second or 'larval' stage in the life of a butterfly or moth, after it has hatched. A caterpillar has a long tube-like body with 13 segments and many legs. It has no wings.

cell
Any area of a butterfly's wing enclosed by veins — but especially the oval cell near the middle of the wing, which is called the discal cell.

chrysalis
The third or 'pupal' stage of many butterflies' lives, when they transform into adults. They often do this inside hard, bean-shaped shells.

cocoon
A bag or shelter spun from silk thread by some caterpillars, especially those of moths, in which they pupate into an adult.

compound eye
The eye of a butterfly or a moth which is made up of many different lenses.

discal cell
See cell.

ecdysis
When caterpillars moult (shed their skin) as they grow, the process is known as ecdysis.

exoskeleton
The hard, outer casing of an insect which acts like a skeleton. It is made of a tough substance called chitin.

food plant
Any particular plant on which a caterpillar feeds.

frenulum
The hook-like bristles that hold the forewing of a moth to its hindwing.

hibernation
A time when an insect is inactive or sleeping during the cold, winter months.

imago
The scientific name for the adult stage in the life of a moth or butterfly, when it has wings.

insect
One of a group of invertebrate animals (ones with no backbone). An insect has three body parts.

instar
A stage in the life of a butterfly or moth between any two moults or dramatic changes. The first instar is the newly hatched caterpillar. After its first moult, it enters the second instar. The final instar is the adult stage.

larva
The scientific name for a caterpillar.

leaf litter
The top layer of a forest floor, consisting of dead and decomposing leaves.

leaf mining
Describes the way that small caterpillars eat tunnels through the insides of leaves.

Lepidoptera
The scientific name for the group of insects made up of butterflies and moths. Lepidoptera comes from Ancient Greek and means "scaly wings".

mandibles
The pair of strong, mouthparts or jaws of a caterpillar.

maxillae
The pair of weaker, lower mouthparts or jaws of an insect.

membrane
A thin skin.

metamorphosis
The series of changes from a caterpillar into an adult.

migration
The regular journeys made by butterflies and moths to follow seasonal changes in the weather.

moulting
A caterpillar grows by shedding its skin periodically and swelling into a new and bigger skin. This is called moulting.

nectar
The sweet juice made by flowers that provides the main food for adult butterflies and moths.

ovipositor
The tube through which a female butterfly or moth pushes her eggs onto a leaf.

palps
Short stalks that project from the mouthparts of a butterfly or moth which act as sense detectors. They play an important part in finding food and food plants.

pheromone
A special chemical released by a butterfly or moth that stimulates another butterfly or moth — especially to mate.

predator
A hunting animal that preys upon others.

proboscis
The long, thin tongue of a butterfly or moth. It is used to suck up nectar from flowers.

puddling
When a butterfly or moth drinks from a muddy pool or puddle.

pupa
The scientific name for the third major stage in the life of a butterfly or moth, when it changes from a caterpillar to an adult — often inside a cocoon. Also known as a chrysalis.

pupation
The change from caterpillar to pupa or chrysalis.

retinaculum
The catch that holds the frenulum. It is used to hook together the forewing and hindwing of a moth.

roosting
Sleeping in a safe place.

scales
The small, thin plates that cover the wing of a butterfly or moth.

sphragis
The horny pouch that male Apollo butterflies ooze onto a female to prevent her mating again.

spinneret
The organ of a caterpillar through which silk emerges.

spiracles
The holes on the side of a caterpillar through which air passes into breathing tubes.

succinct pupa
A pupa or chrysalis that is held pointing upwards by a silken thread.

suspended pupa
A pupa or chrysalis that is hanging down from a small pad of silk.

tarsi
The feet of a butterfly or moth. The tarsi often contain important taste organs.

thorax
The middle part of the three body sections of an insect. The thorax is packed with strong muscles that move the wings and legs.

tympanal organs
The "ears" on the abdomen or thorax of an insect. The tympanal organs are made up of small holes, each one covered by a membrane.

veins
The supporting framework of the wing of a butterfly or moth. The pattern of veins (venation) is often used to classify butterflies and moths.

venation
See veins.

INDEX